DEDICATION

COPYRIGHT

Paperback ISBN: 978-1-990391-14-9
eBook ISBN: 978-1-989939-12-3
First Published September 2021
Book design, cover design, and illustrations by Mei Yu.

For business inquiries, please contact Mei Yu.

Cozy Ombre Dress

BY MEI YU

1.
Since we'll focus on drawing clothes, the body is just for our reference.

First, draw a cozy scarf wrapped around her neck. Then, draw the skirt part of the dress like a cone.

Learn to draw bodies in detail in my other books *How to Draw Famous Characters as Princesses* and *How to Draw Social Media as Models*.

2.
Draw more curves in the scarf to show the soft folds, then draw the top of the dress that fits closely around her front and arms.

Draw leggings after.

3.
Draw fine folds in the skirt. The more you add, the more detailed and refined the fabric looks. Try varying the lengths of the folds for a more natural look.

Then, draw a cute pattern in her leggings, like little cat head shapes!

Cozy Ombre Dress

BY MEI YU

4.
Erase extra lines, then use a dark pen or marker to go over the final lines!

If you have a thin-tipped pen, try that to ink the finer details in your drawing like the fabric folds or the legging pattern.

This is a beautiful outfit for autumn! Try this look for your character when she's walking under brilliant trees with falling leaves. Or, she could be on a cute date!

Throughout this book, you will see how various outfits can make a character look different.

After, expand your design skills even further with the male version in *Draw 1 Boy in 20 Outfits - Fall*. The more you draw, the better you draw!

BY MEI YU

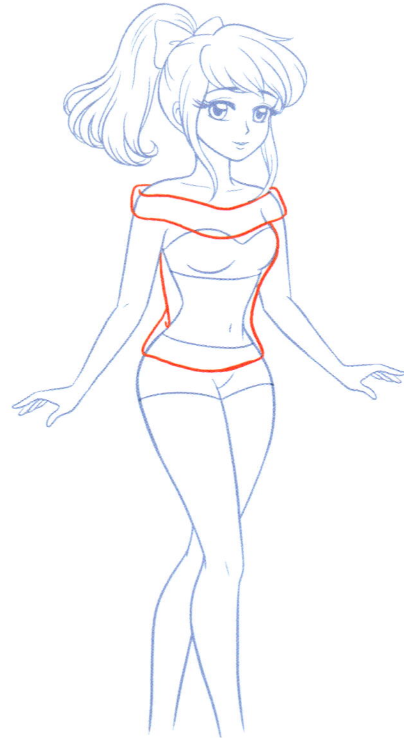

1.
Make the collar of her sweater go across her shoulders. Then, draw the sides as loose lines.

Keep the edge curved around the waist for a dimensional look.

2.
Draw sleeves that fit closely along her arms. Add a cute pumpkin design, then draw shorts.

Add ovals as holes in her leggings.

3.
Draw lines in her collar for texture. This is a good way to make sweaters look more woolen and cozy.

Add details in her shorts, including the torn edges. For leggings, draw them close to the legs, with some creases in the fabric around the holes.

BY MEI YU

4.
Use a dark pen or marker to go over the lines you want to keep. When inking, try to keep your wrist loose so the lines will not be too stiff.

This is a great outfit for characters who are into Halloween. It's also a little edgy, so try this for characters who have a personality to match.

For more outfit ideas and tutorials, see my books *How to Draw Social Media as Models* and *How to Draw Villains as Princesses*.

BY MEI YU

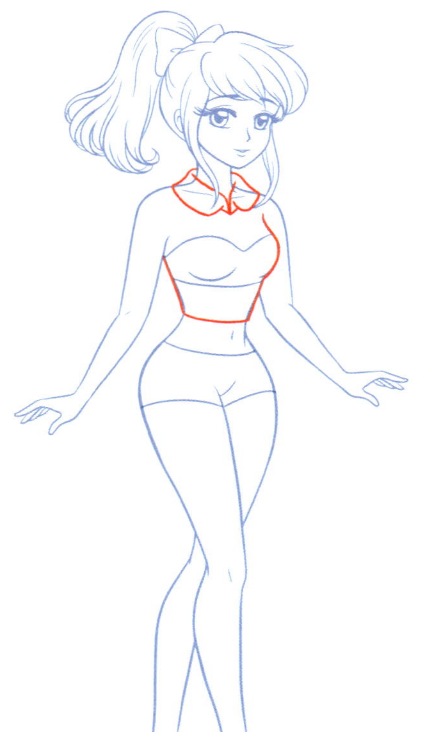

1.
Begin with her collar like two rectangles facing each other. Then, draw part of the top of the dress. It fits closely on her body.

2.
Add the long skirt that ends at the knees as a soft cone. Draw the sleeves short and slightly puffy.

Add folds in the fabric to show the curve of the body underneath.

3.
Make the edges of her collar cute with little waves to make a curly edge.

Do the same with the sleeves. Draw some wrinkles near the waist to show the waist part is snug around her. For the bottom edge of the dress, draw some decorative curves.

BY MEI YU

4.
Use your choice of a dark pen or marker to go over the final lines.

The nice contrast between the dark and light areas of this dress is eye-catching. It helps create a classy, more sophisticated look for your character. You can also try your own color combinations!

This dress can be good for a character who is attending a formal event, having afternoon tea, or reading a book with a cozy fireplace nearby.

BY MEI YU

1.
Start her dress with the top part that fits around her body.

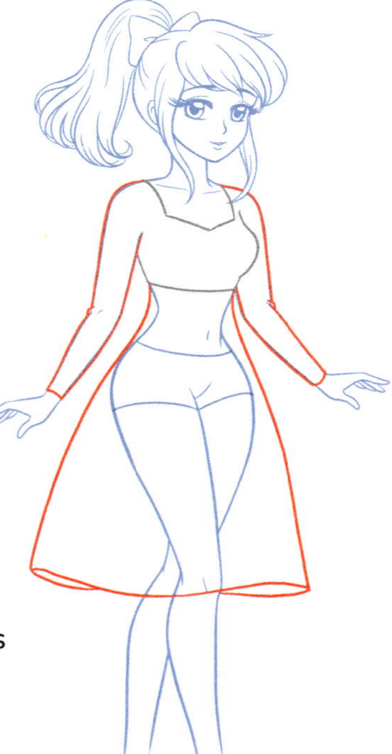

2.
The dress is tight under her bust, then flows loosely down past her knees. It looks like a curved triangle.

Add slim-fitting sleeves.

3.
Draw wrinkles in her outfit, then start a pattern of leaf shapes.

Try tilting them in various ways for a more interesting look. This helps add a sense of movement to the design.

4.
Fill the bottom part of the dress with smaller leaves. It looks like lots of leaves falling from the sky.

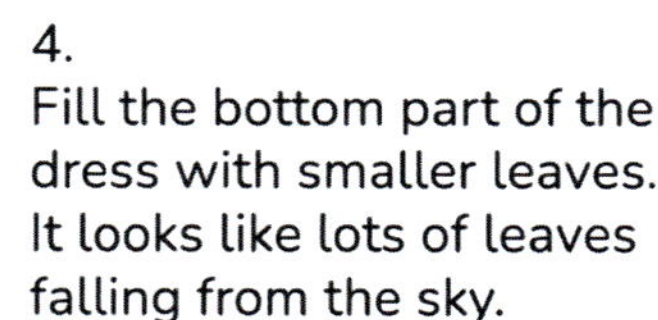

Elegant Leaves Dress

BY MEI YU

5.
Erase extra lines, then finalize your drawing.

Try to use a thin-tipped pen to ink the delicate leaf patterns.

This beautiful dress can bring a warm autumn feeling! Try this dress with girls who are nature lovers or who love the fall season.

Learn to draw other dresses for your OCs in my books *How to Draw Famous Characters as Princesses* and *How to Draw Social Media as Models*. The more you draw, the better you draw!

BY MEI YU

1.
Start her loose sweater with soft lines. Leave space between the sides of the sweater and her body to show the loose fit.

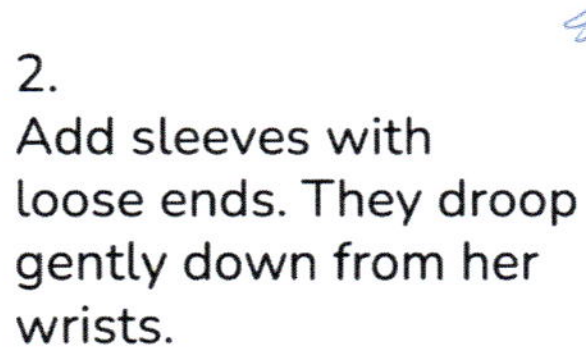

2.
Add sleeves with loose ends. They droop gently down from her wrists.

Then, start her cute skirt sides with short lines that hug her hips.

3.
Draw the skirt as a wide curve, with stylish folds.

Then, draw lines in the collar of the sweater for a woolen look.

4.
Add the curved edges of the skirt, then draw her leggings.

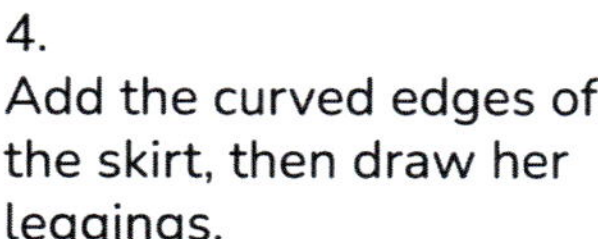

BY MEI YU

5.
Erase extra lines before finalizing your drawing with a dark pen.

This outfit is a nice choice for a character who might be in informal situations, like hanging out with her girlfriends, or walking her pet in the park! She could have an energetic personality, who is bubbly and bright.

BY MEI YU

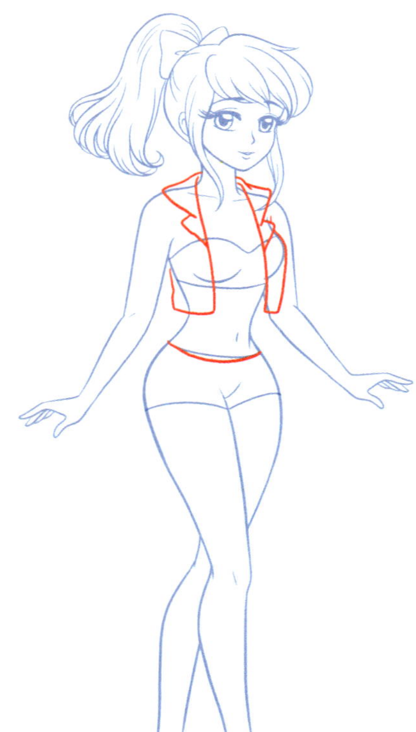

1.
Start her jacket with the front opening.

Draw the collar pieces as two triangles on either side.

Add a curved line for the shirt edge around the waist.

2.
Draw the sleeves of the jacket. For the shirt under the jacket, draw a V-neck collar, and the shirt sides.

Add wrinkles around the chest to show the fabric creases.

3.
Draw skinny jeans with lines fitting closely along the legs.

BY MEI YU

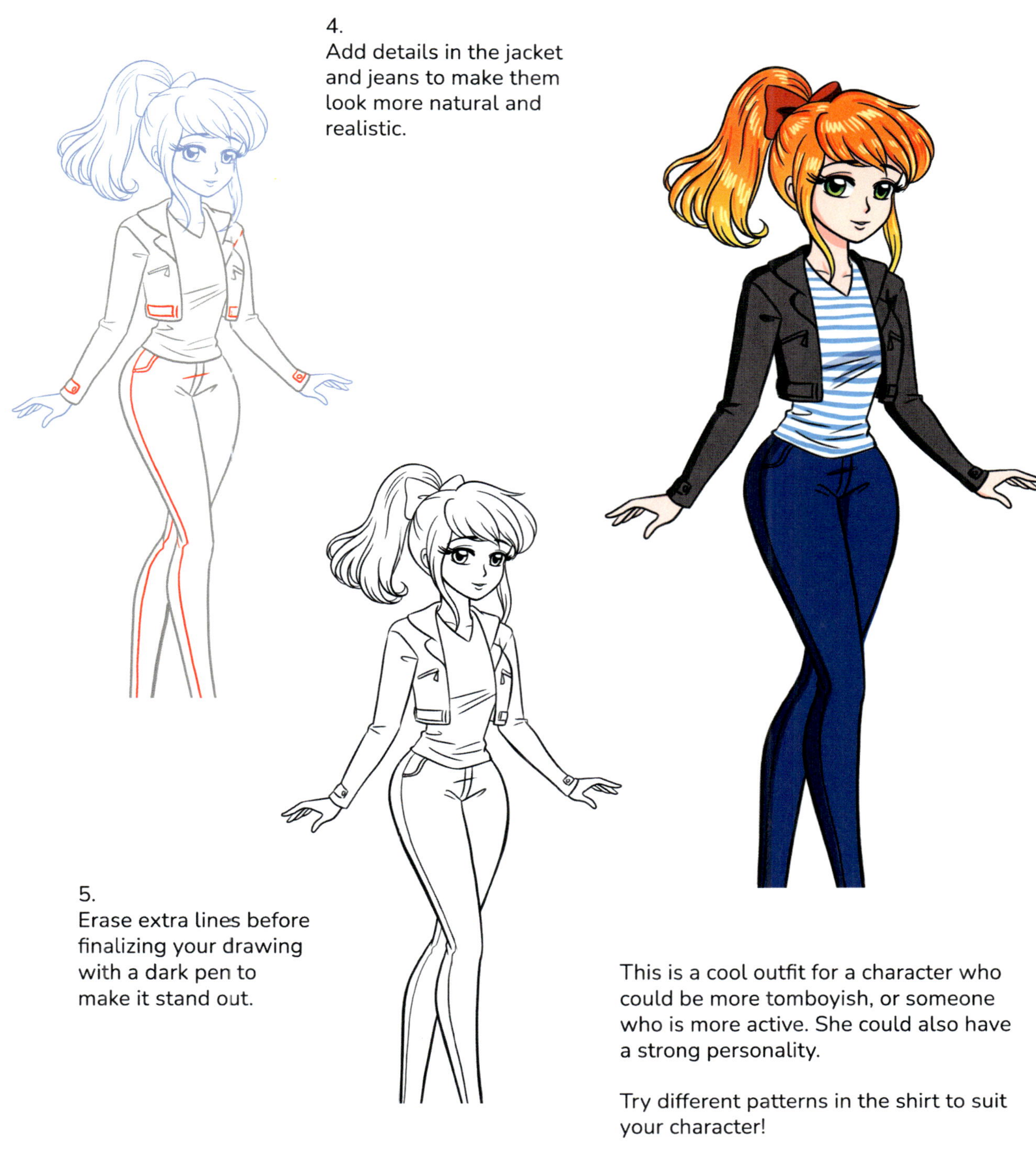

4.
Add details in the jacket and jeans to make them look more natural and realistic.

5.
Erase extra lines before finalizing your drawing with a dark pen to make it stand out.

This is a cool outfit for a character who could be more tomboyish, or someone who is more active. She could also have a strong personality.

Try different patterns in the shirt to suit your character!

BY MEI YU

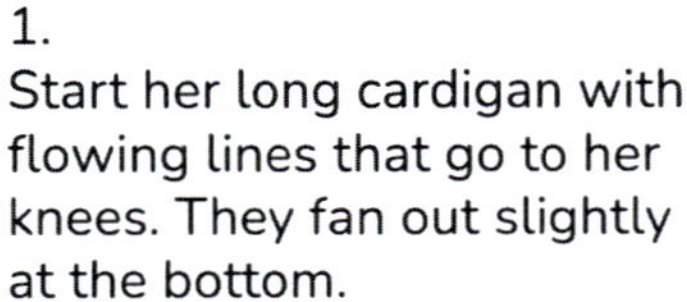

1.
Start her long cardigan with flowing lines that go to her knees. They fan out slightly at the bottom.

Draw her thin scarf that covers her front.

2.
Draw her sleeves fitted and rolled at the elbows.

Then, draw her stylish shorts with a high waist and buttons.

3.
Draw folds in her shirt and cardigan. Add leggings.

For her scarf, draw small lines along the triangular edge for a fringe effect.

BY MEI YU

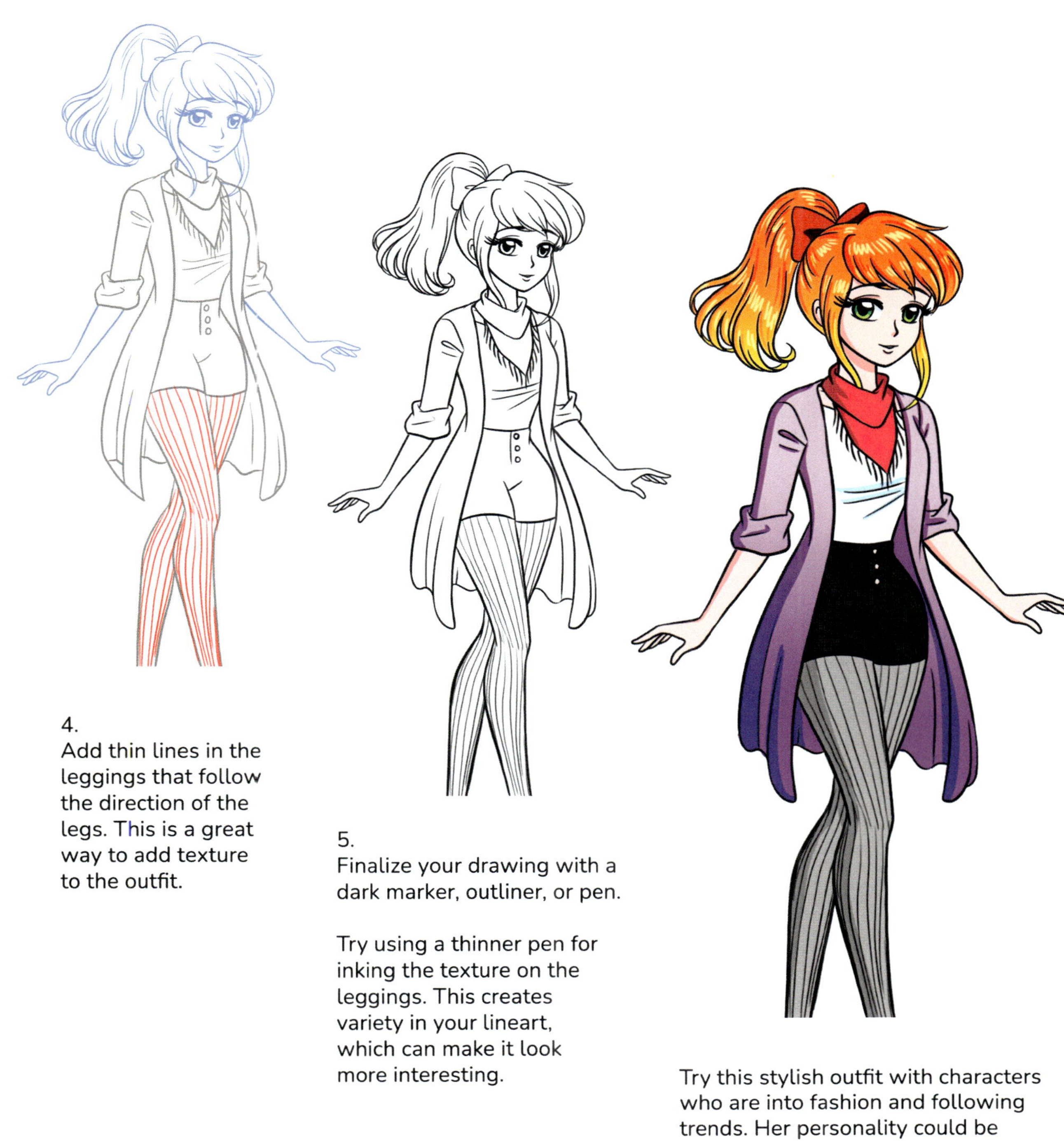

4.
Add thin lines in the leggings that follow the direction of the legs. This is a great way to add texture to the outfit.

5.
Finalize your drawing with a dark marker, outliner, or pen.

Try using a thinner pen for inking the texture on the leggings. This creates variety in your lineart, which can make it look more interesting.

Try this stylish outfit with characters who are into fashion and following trends. Her personality could be confident, sassy, or outgoing.

BY MEI YU

1.
Draw her cute scarf tied to one side. Then, draw the top closely fitted along her body.

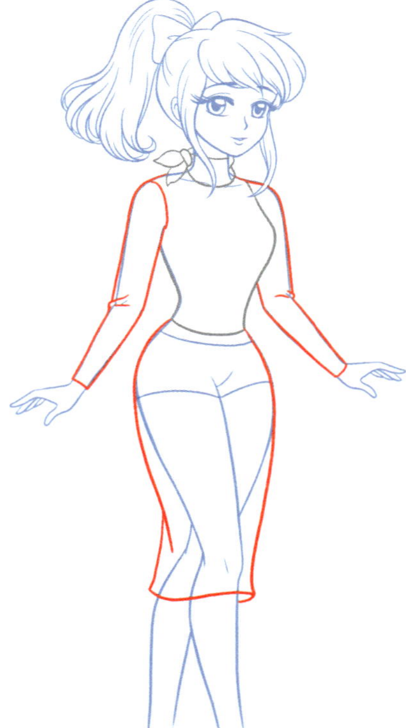

2.
Add curved lines that go down past her knees for her skirt. The fabric is loose, so keep some distance between her legs and the skirt lines.

Draw fitted sleeves after.

3.
Draw her knitted collar and edge for her vest on top. Add folds in the fabric to make the clothing softer.

Fall Pattern Outfit

BY MEI YU

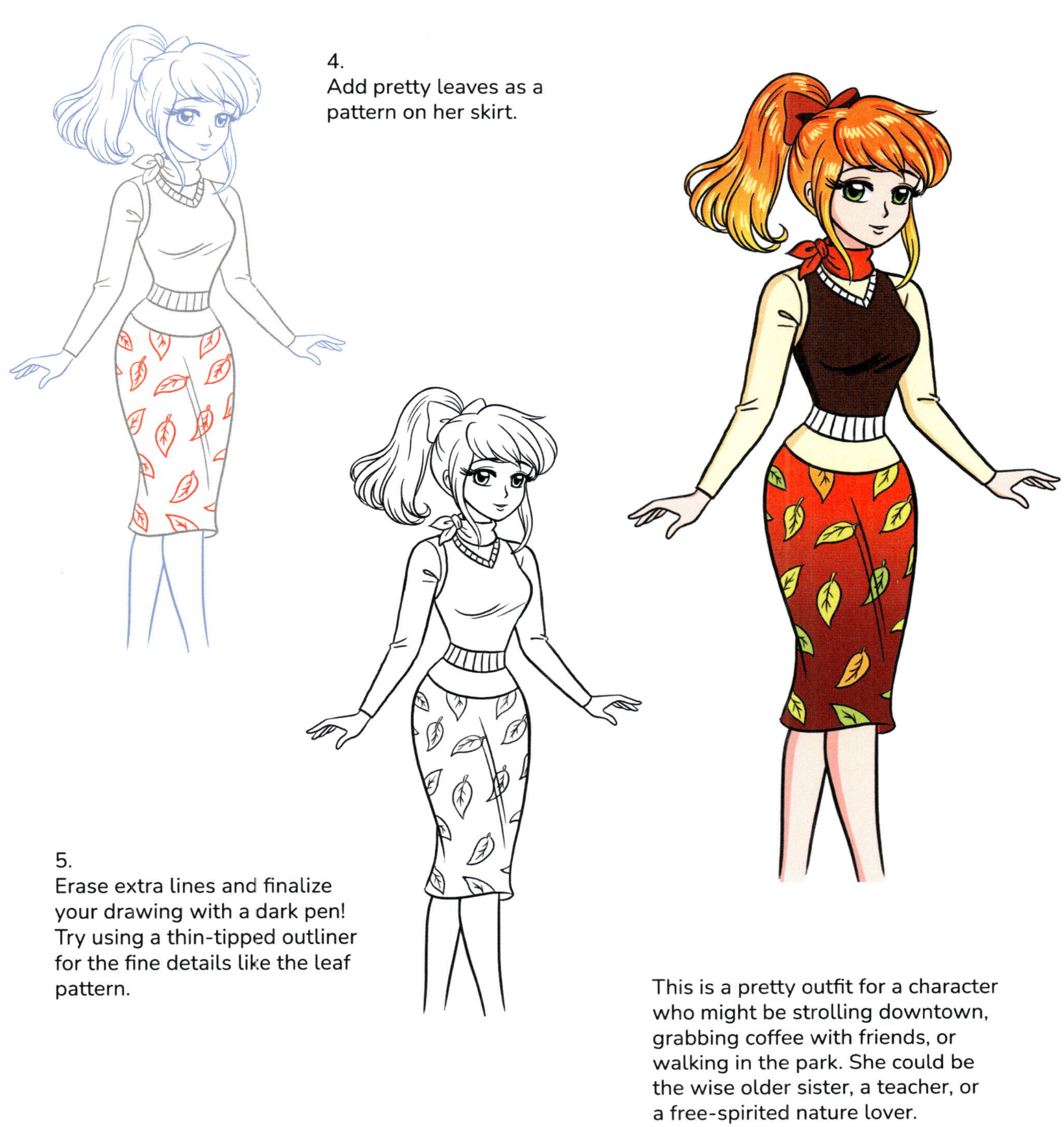

4.
Add pretty leaves as a pattern on her skirt.

5.
Erase extra lines and finalize your drawing with a dark pen! Try using a thin-tipped outliner for the fine details like the leaf pattern.

This is a pretty outfit for a character who might be strolling downtown, grabbing coffee with friends, or walking in the park. She could be the wise older sister, a teacher, or a free-spirited nature lover.

Casual Office Look

BY MEI YU

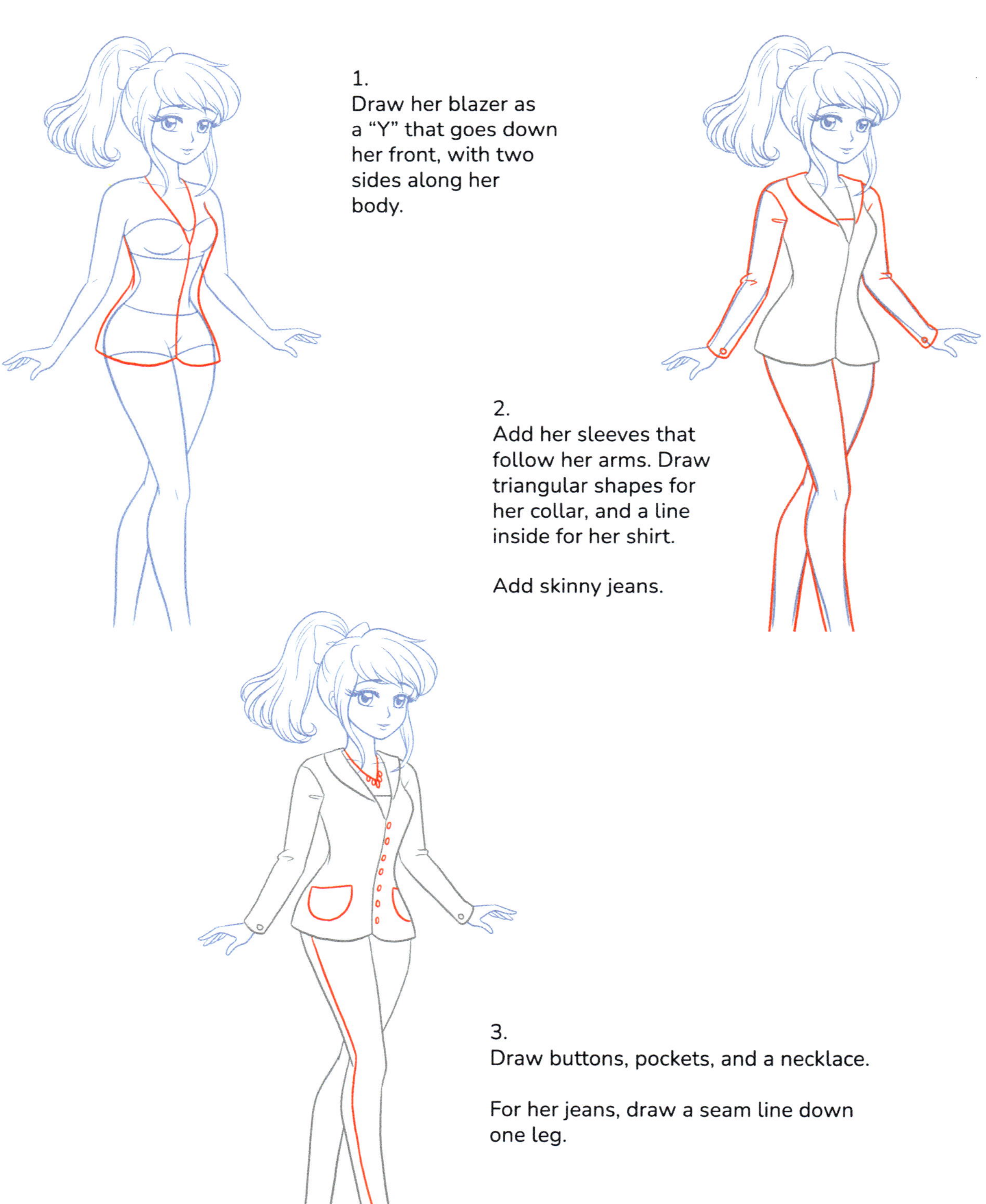

1.
Draw her blazer as a "Y" that goes down her front, with two sides along her body.

2.
Add her sleeves that follow her arms. Draw triangular shapes for her collar, and a line inside for her shirt.

Add skinny jeans.

3.
Draw buttons, pockets, and a necklace.

For her jeans, draw a seam line down one leg.

BY MEI YU

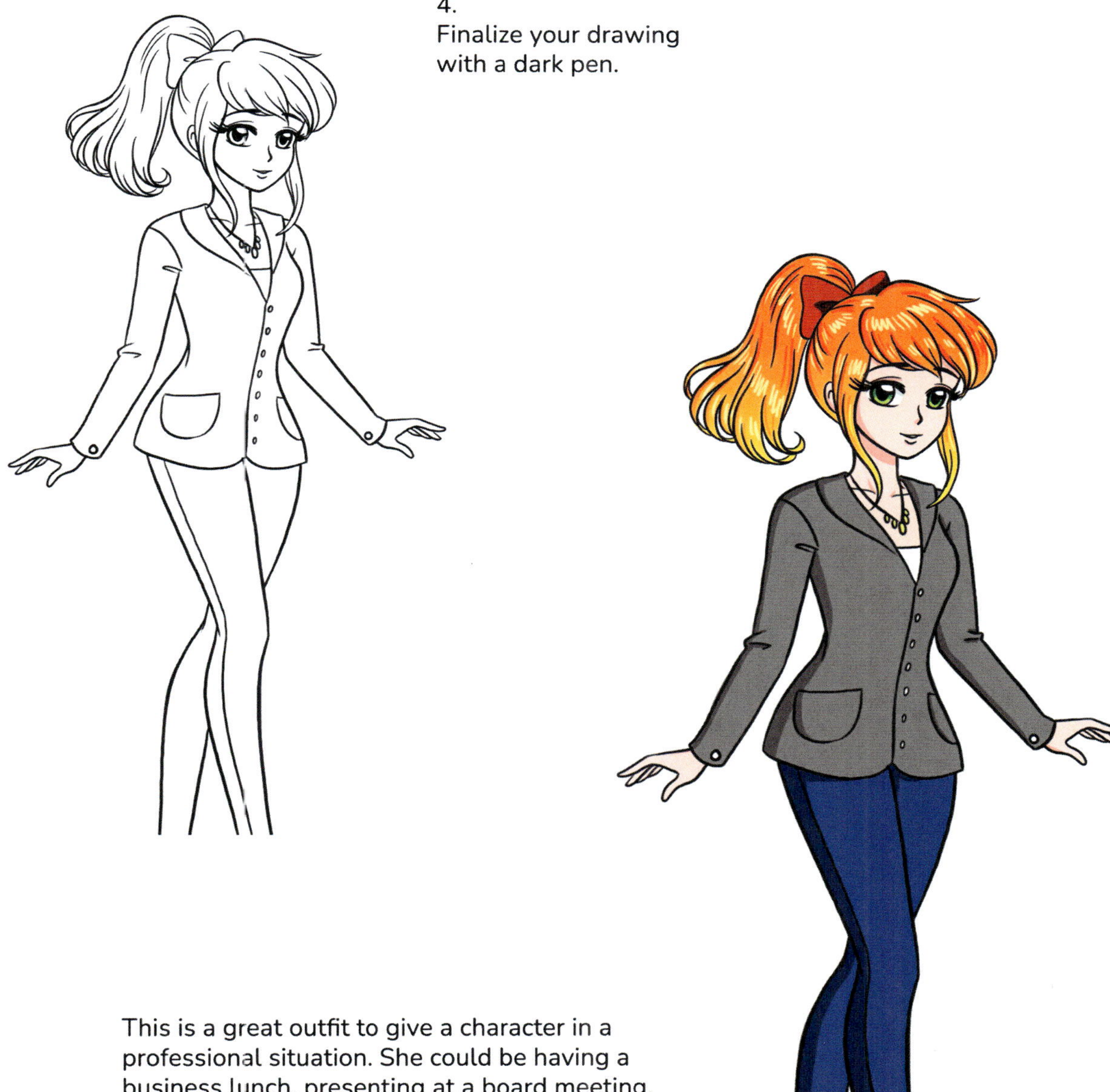

4.
Finalize your drawing
with a dark pen.

This is a great outfit to give a character in a
professional situation. She could be having a
business lunch, presenting at a board meeting,
or showing off her fancy startup to her friends!

Draw the cool male version in my companion
book *Draw 1 Boy in 20 Outfits - Fall*.

BY MEI YU

1.
Draw a bow on her front, with her collar.

Then, add a curved band around her waist.

2.
Add the sides of the top, going into the tapered waist in the middle. Draw puffy sleeves and a skirt.

3.
Add folds in the skirt. Draw stripes in the collar and sleeve edges. To make the fabric look soft, add wrinkles.

Add her knee-high socks.

BY MEI YU

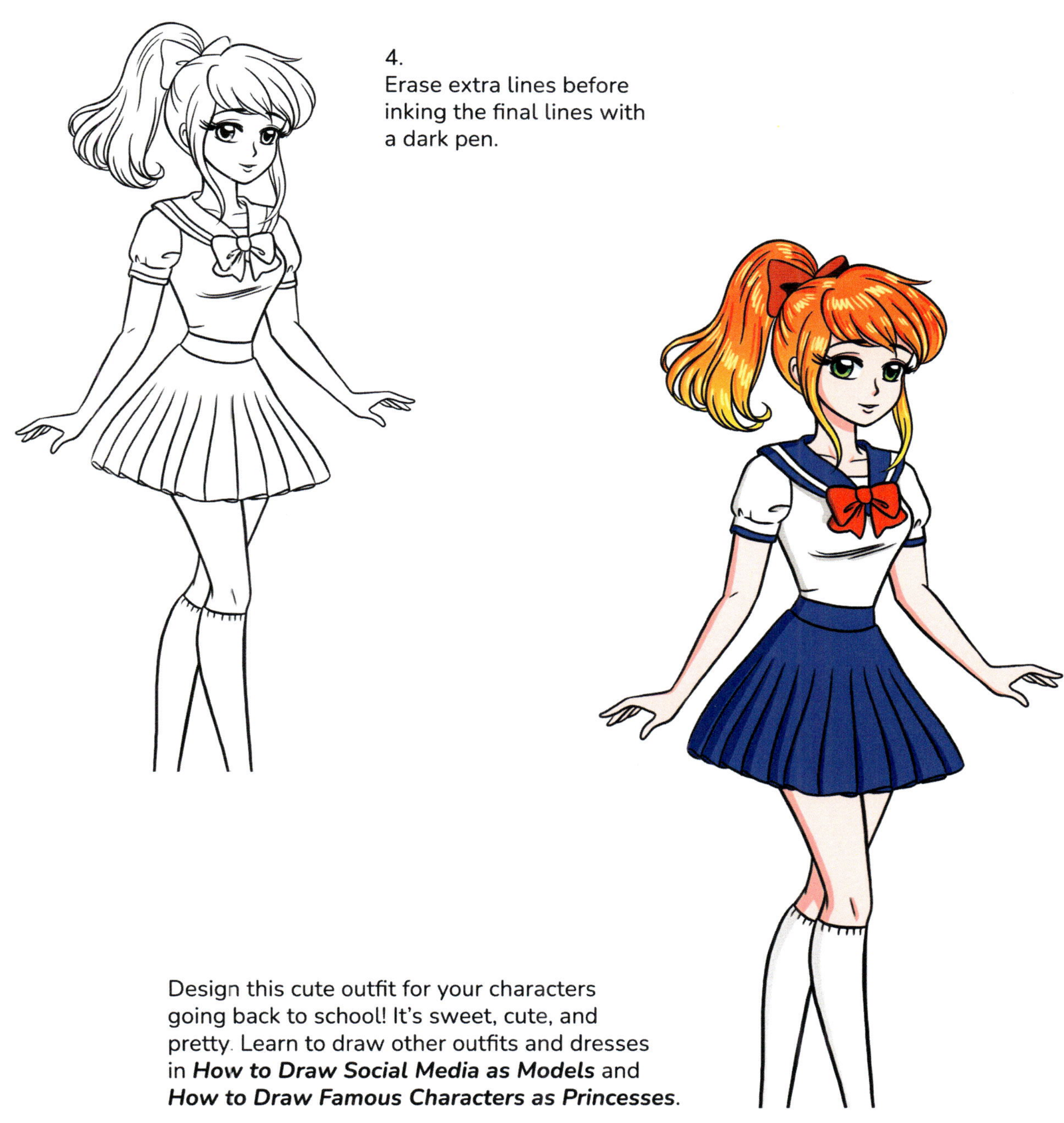

4.
Erase extra lines before inking the final lines with a dark pen.

Design this cute outfit for your characters going back to school! It's sweet, cute, and pretty. Learn to draw other outfits and dresses in *How to Draw Social Media as Models* and *How to Draw Famous Characters as Princesses*.

Cute Fall Outfit

BY MEI YU

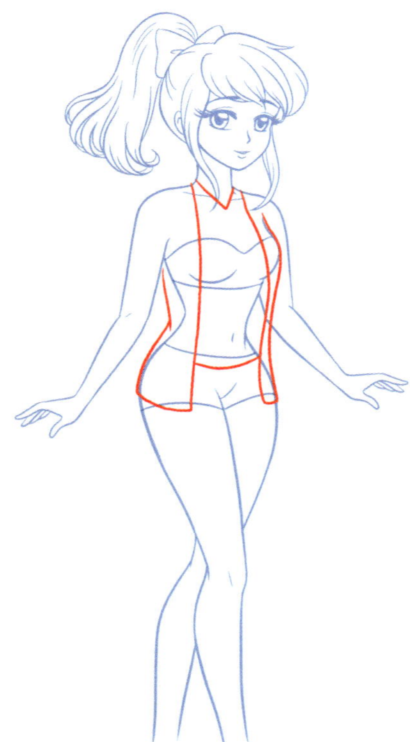

1.
Begin with her cardigan open. Then, draw a V-neck for her shirt underneath.

2.
Draw her sleeves that end at her elbows.

For her shirt, draw a collar, then a line down the middle of her body.

After, draw form-fitting pants.

3.
Draw a pretty necklace, then some wrinkles in her cardigan, shirt, and pants.

Cute Fall Outfit

BY MEI YU

4.
Erase extra lines. After, to make your drawing stand out, finalize your drawing with your choice of a dark pen, marker, or outliner.

This outfit is versatile! It's great for characters who are in an office situation, hanging out with friends, or on a cute date walking through falling leaves in a tranquil forest.

Pretty Activewear

BY MEI YU

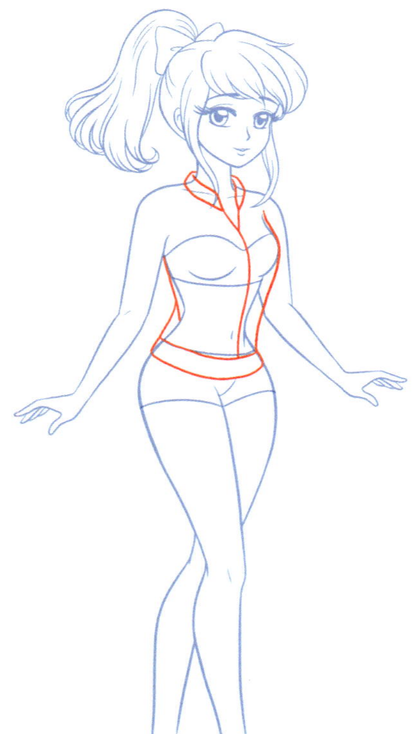

1.
Draw her jacket with the collar and zipper like a long "Y" down her front. Add the loose sides.

2.
Draw her sleeves with rolled ends at her elbows.

Her leggings end below the knees.

3.
Add a stripe down her sleeves. Then, draw pockets and wrinkles in her jacket.

For her leggings, add a simple design like diagonal stripes. These will provide more areas for you to color in.

BY MEI YU

4.
Finalize your drawing with a dark pen or marker!

Design this outfit for sporty, athletic characters! She could be doing yoga, hiking, or jogging. Your character could also go running with her pet or boyfriend.

Draw the handsome male version of this outfit for her boyfriend in my companion book *Draw 1 Boy in 20 Outfits - Fall*.

Pretty in Polka Dots

BY MEI YU

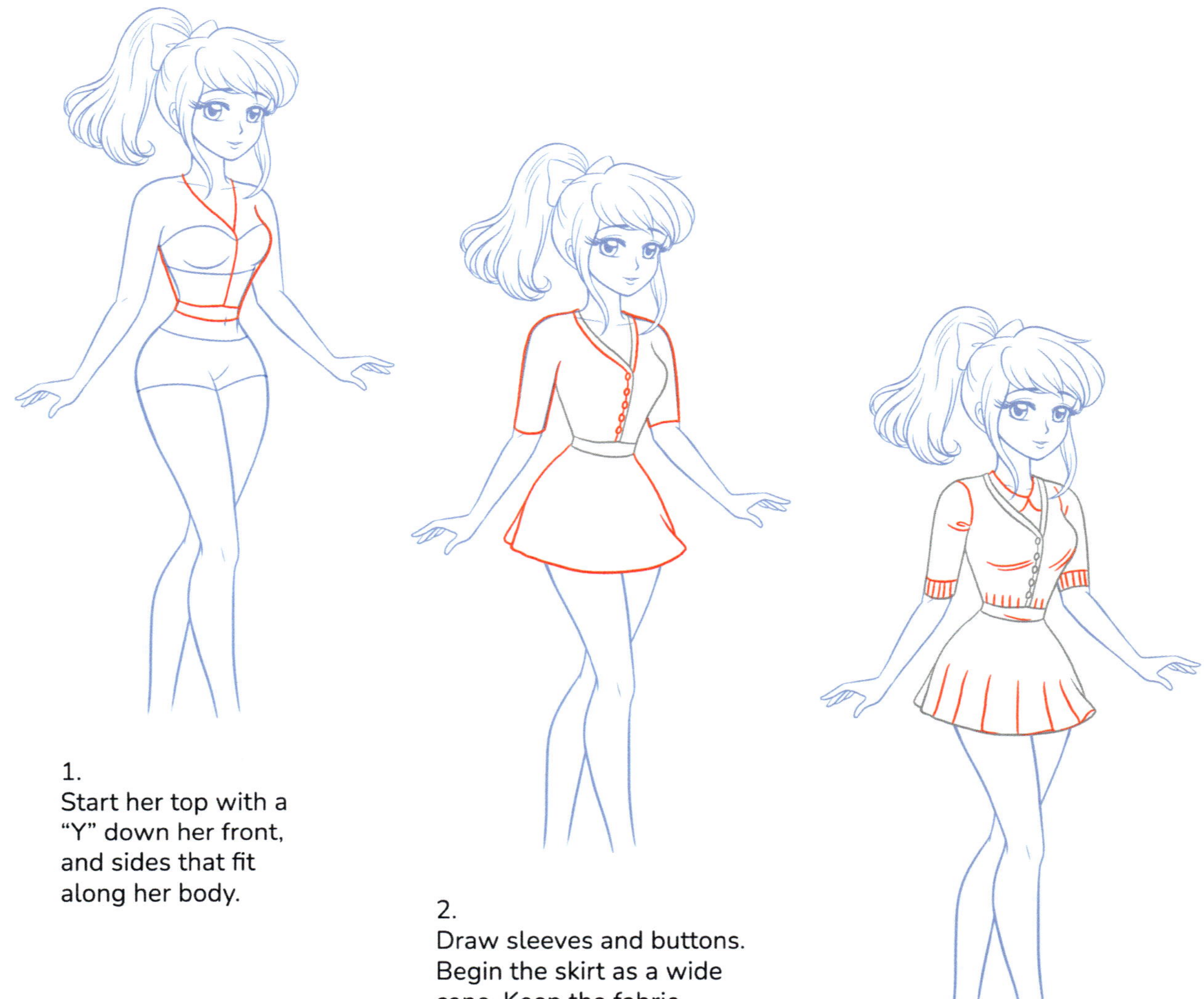

1.
Start her top with a "Y" down her front, and sides that fit along her body.

2.
Draw sleeves and buttons. Begin the skirt as a wide cone. Keep the fabric looking soft with some folds in the skirt.

3.
Add more details in the clothing with folds and wrinkles.

Draw a little collar underneath for another layer.

BY MEI YU

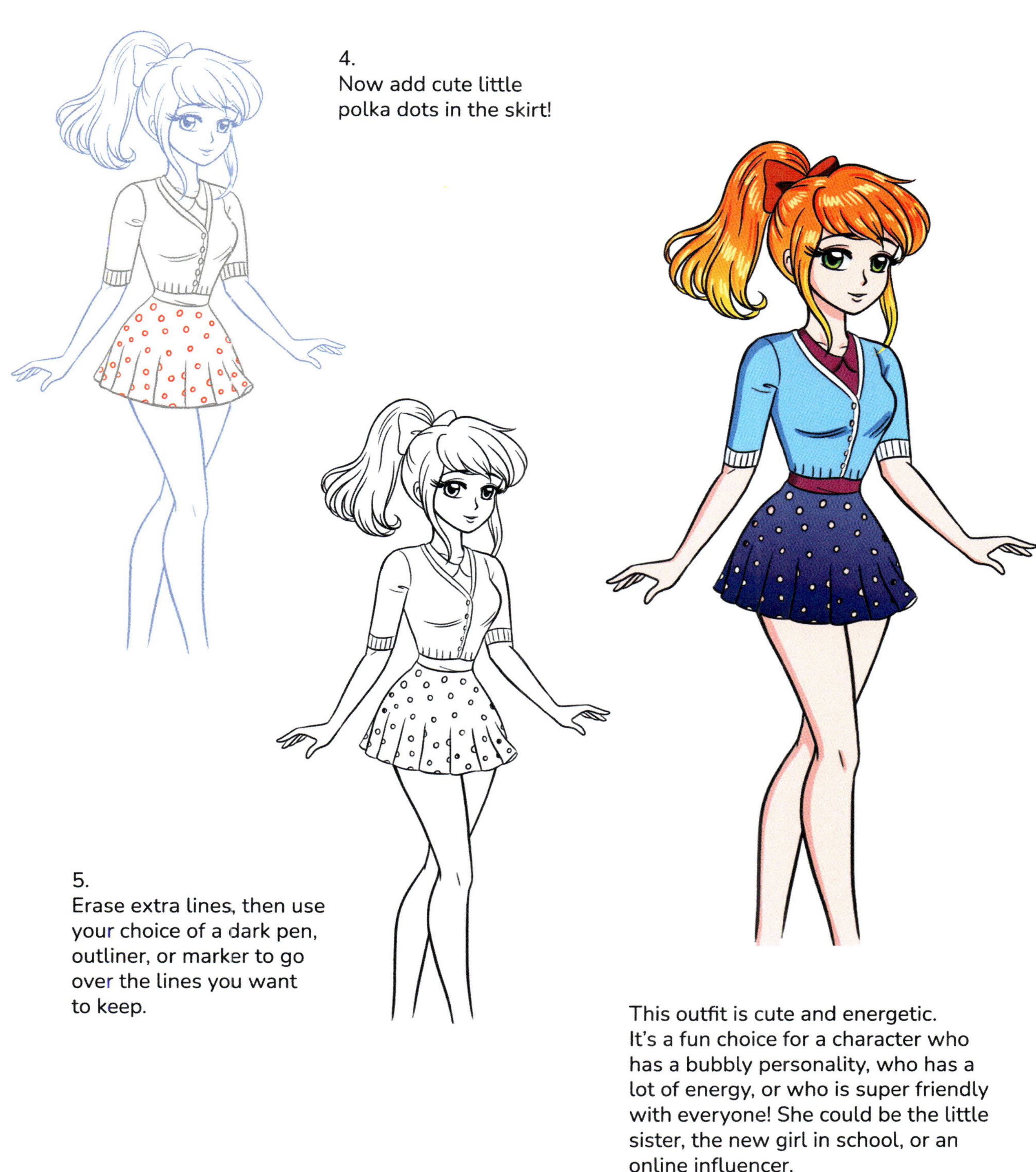

4.
Now add cute little polka dots in the skirt!

5.
Erase extra lines, then use your choice of a dark pen, outliner, or marker to go over the lines you want to keep.

This outfit is cute and energetic. It's a fun choice for a character who has a bubbly personality, who has a lot of energy, or who is super friendly with everyone! She could be the little sister, the new girl in school, or an online influencer.

BY MEI YU

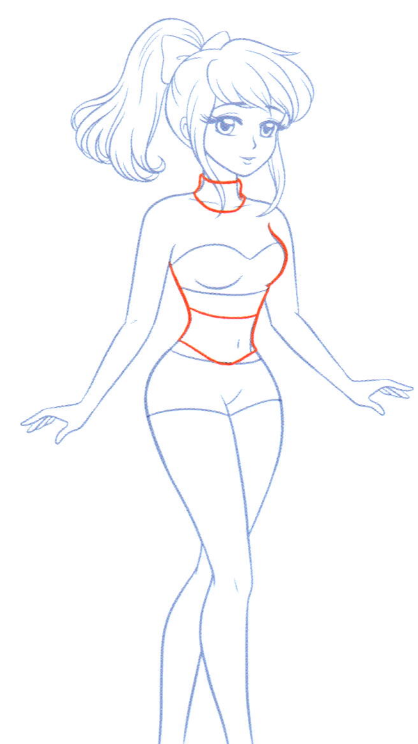

1.
Draw a curved shape around her neck for the turtleneck of her top.

Then, add the sides of the top going along her body.

2.
Add sleeves that open up slightly at the wrists.

Her skirt is form-fitting. Use curved lines to make the fabric soft.

3.
Add lines in the waist for a nice texture. This also makes the waist part of her clothing look like it's closely wrapped around her. Keep her leggings tight by drawing lines that are going along her legs.

BY MEI YU

4.
Finalize your drawing
to make it stand out!

Try giving this outfit to characters who are stylish, well-mannered, or wealthy. She could be someone who prefers simple, yet fashionable looks. She could also be someone who is the more mature, older sister type whom others rely on for advice.

The color scheme of her outfit suggests she's more grounded, as the colors aren't too wild. Experiment with different combinations to suit your character.

Learn to draw hairstyles for posh or elegant characters and others with *Draw 1 Girl with 20 Hairstyles*.
Keep drawing!

BY MEI YU

1.
Begin with the loose opening of her sweater coming down one shoulder in a cool off-shoulder look.

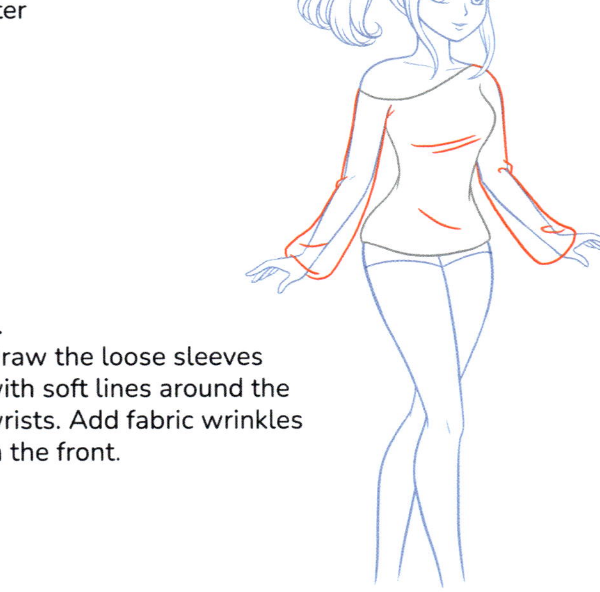

2.
Draw the loose sleeves with soft lines around the wrists. Add fabric wrinkles in the front.

3.
Draw her pants fitted along the lines of her legs. For a more casual look, make them rolled up under the knees. Draw the rolled parts like curved rectangles around her legs.

A good way to make the parts of the body and clothing look dimensional is to draw the clothing following the roundness of the body with curved lines.

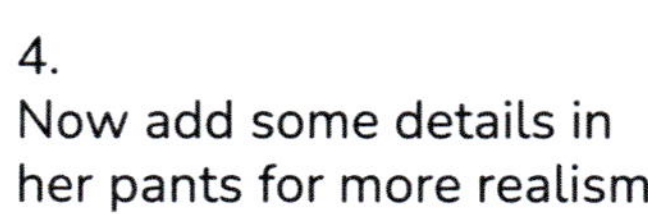

4.
Now add some details in her pants for more realism.

BY MEI YU

5.
Go over your final lines
to ink your drawing.

This casual look is fun for a character who is hanging at a friend's home, going for a quick bite to eat, or relaxing under the stars with her crush.

For other cute off-shoulder looks, try my book *Draw 1 Girl in 20 Outfits - Summer*.

Sweet + Kawaii

BY MEI YU

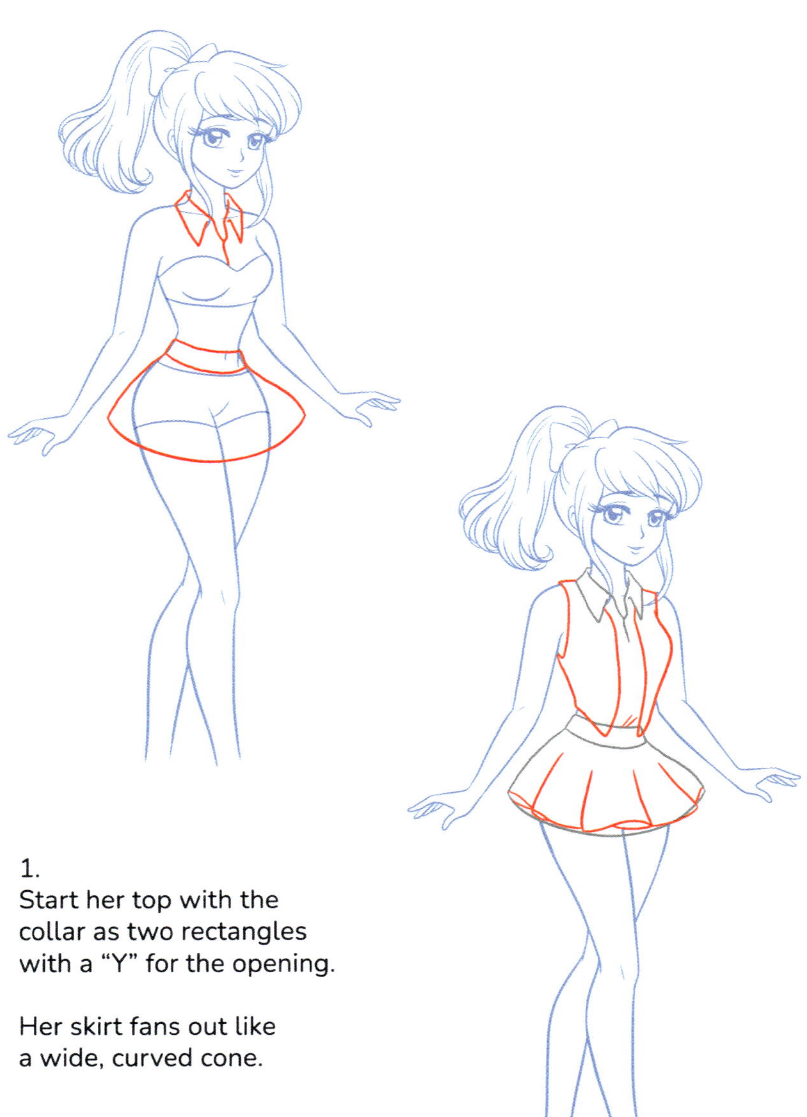

1.
Start her top with the collar as two rectangles with a "Y" for the opening.

Her skirt fans out like a wide, curved cone.

2.
Draw a short vest opened on top. For her skirt, draw short folds and the wavy edge.

3.
Draw short sleeves with soft rectangles for rolled-up ends.

Add small wrinkles in her shirt and skirt. Then, add her leggings that closely follow her legs.

BY MEI YU

4.
After erasing extra lines,
use a dark pen or marker
to finalize your drawing.

This character could be sweet, innocent,
or young. She could also be a fan of
anything and everything cute and kawaii!

Your character could be into fandoms,
moe culture, or cosplaying! To make her
look more "soft and gentle," try pastel
colors for her outfit.

BY MEI YU

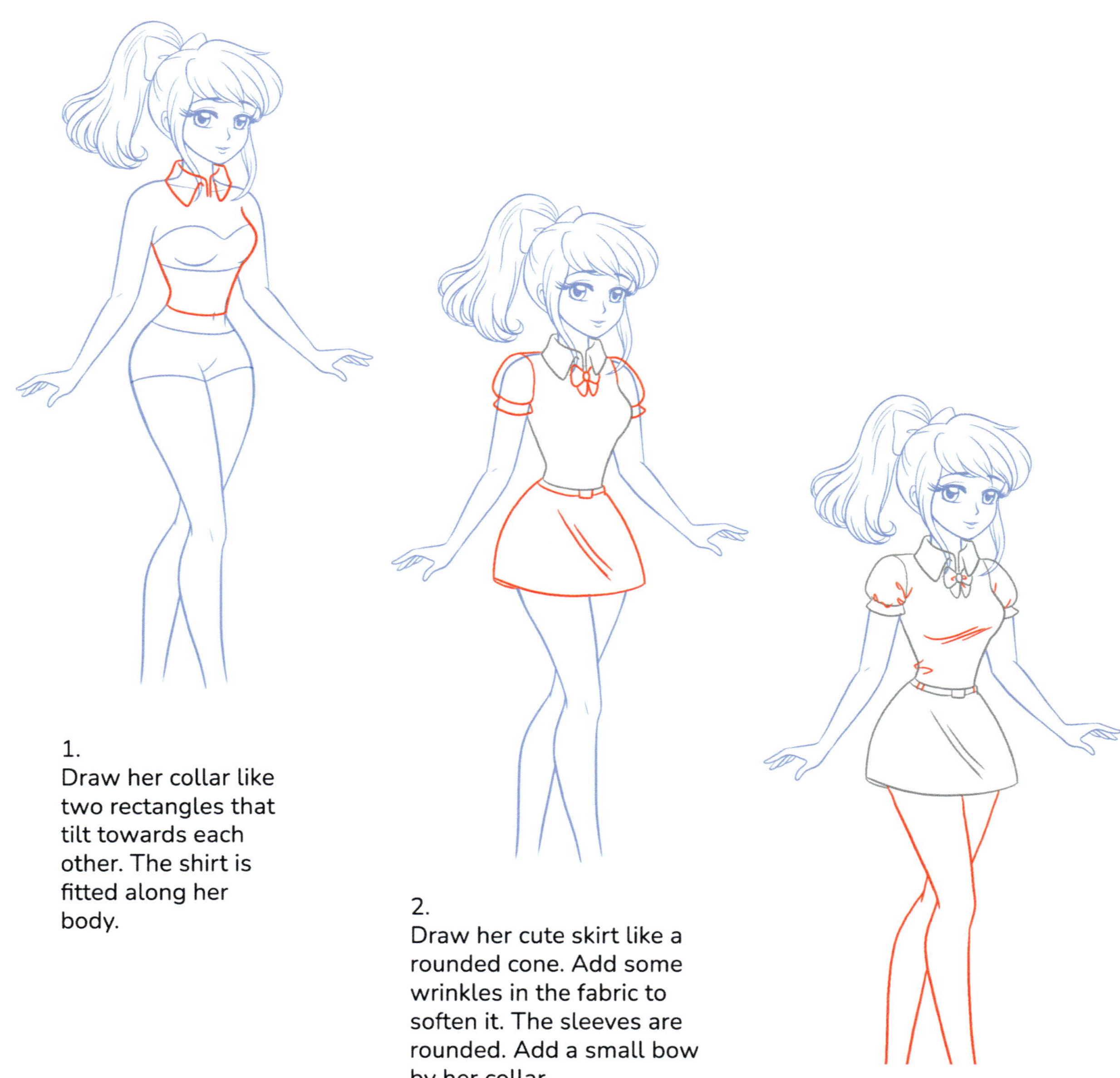

1.
Draw her collar like two rectangles that tilt towards each other. The shirt is fitted along her body.

2.
Draw her cute skirt like a rounded cone. Add some wrinkles in the fabric to soften it. The sleeves are rounded. Add a small bow by her collar.

3.
Draw her leggings tight around her legs. Draw some wrinkles in major areas to show the structure of the body underneath.

BY MEI YU

4.
Erase extra lines if needed, then ink your art!

This is a cute outfit to give characters who are energetic, spunky, or a little nerdy. She could be a bookworm who loves reading by a fireplace, or a student watching a romantic sunset with her crush.

Try designing more outfits for your OCs with the summer and winter editions of *Draw 1 Girl in 20 Outfits*. Those other outfits can give you lots of good ideas to incorporate into your designs for any season! You can apply the skills you learn in other situations.

Hoodie Outfit

BY MEI YU

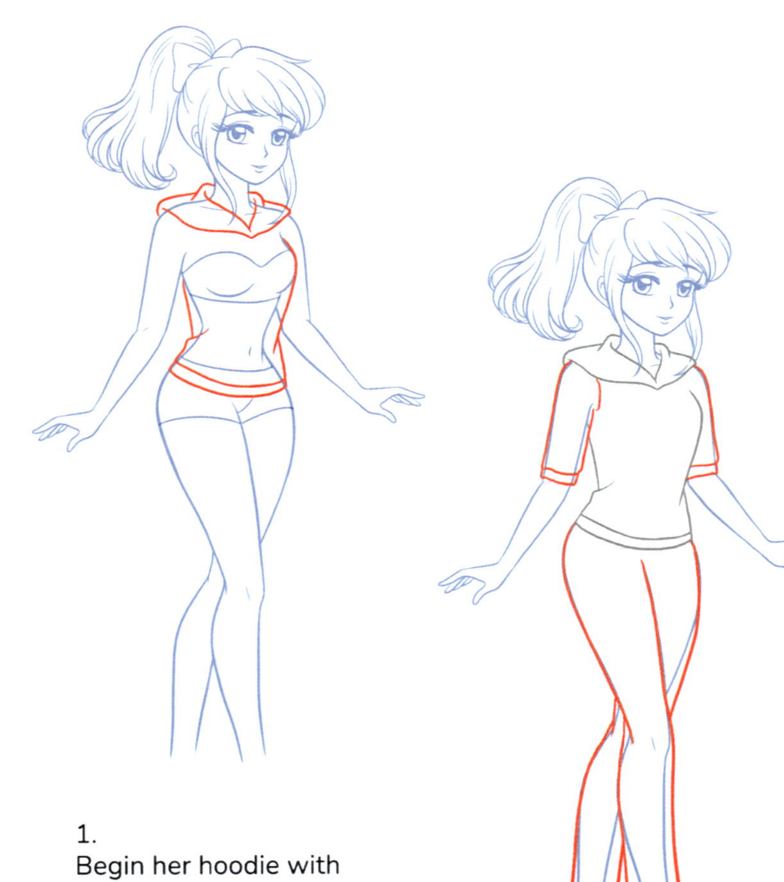

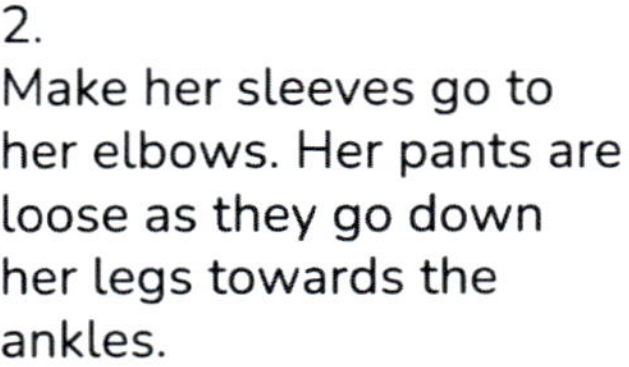

1.
Begin her hoodie with the triangular hood part by her neck.

Make the sides loose down her body.

2.
Make her sleeves go to her elbows. Her pants are loose as they go down her legs towards the ankles.

3.
Draw the front pocket of her hoodie, some wrinkles around her arms and front, then the drawstrings.

Add details in her pants like wrinkles and the seam lines.

BY MEI YU

4.
Erase extra lines and use a dark pen to finalize your drawing.

This cute outfit is great for a character in casual situations. She could also be sporty, tomboyish, or spunky.

Beautiful Long Dress

BY MEI YU

1.
Draw her top connected at her front. Then, draw her shirt underneath that's fitted along her body.

2.
Draw her sleeves for the top layer. Add some wrinkles. Then, make her dress long with flowing lines. It looks like a soft triangle.

3.
Add wrinkles in the dress to soften the fabric.

Make your outfit more interesting and detailed with fancy designs!

BY MEI YU

4.
Erase extra lines and
finalize your art with
a dark pen.

She looks warm and elegant! This look can
be for a character who is from a village or
town. She could also be artistic, creative,
or the type who loves handmade things.

Practice drawing other graceful dresses in
How to Draw Social Media as Models and
How to Draw Famous Characters as Princesses.

BY MEI YU

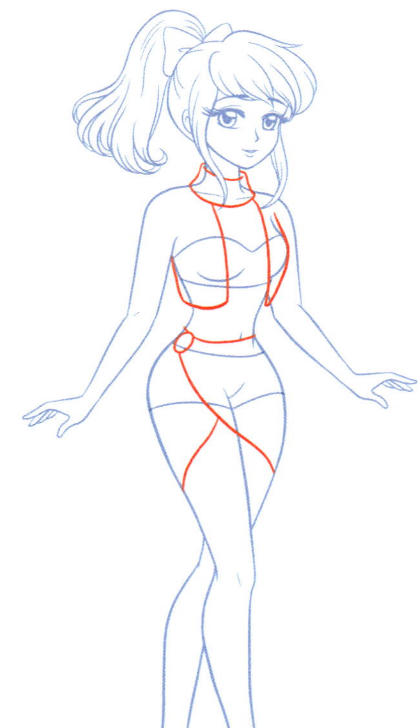

1.
Start her cropped jacket with the opened front. Draw her curved collar, then basic lines for her pretty skirt.

2.
Add sleeves, a necklace, and the sides of her skirt.

3.
Draw lines in her collar to make it more stylish. Add her shirt under the jacket, and then her leggings.

BY MEI YU

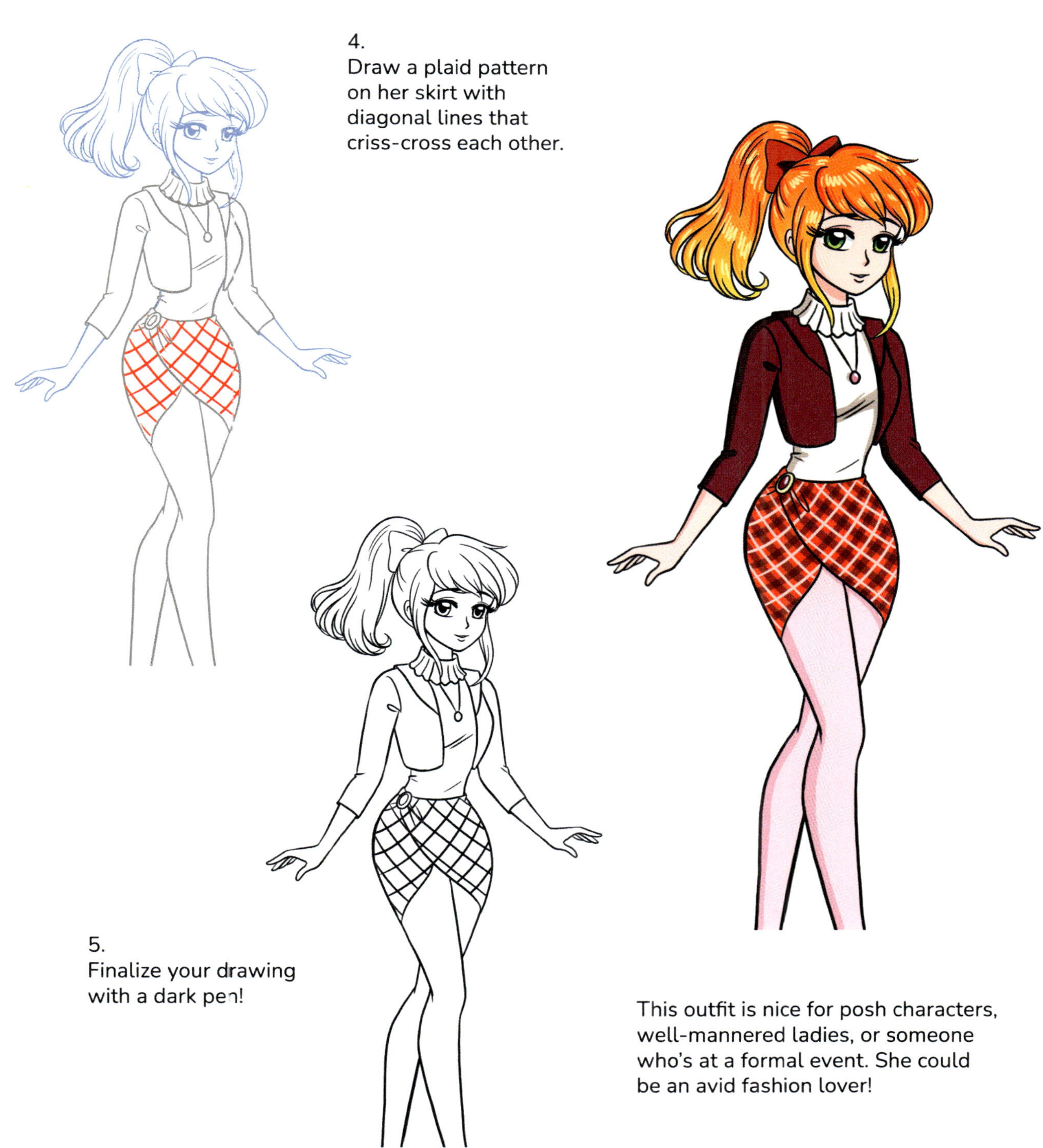

4.
Draw a plaid pattern on her skirt with diagonal lines that criss-cross each other.

5.
Finalize your drawing with a dark pen!

This outfit is nice for posh characters, well-mannered ladies, or someone who's at a formal event. She could be an avid fashion lover!

eBooks

★ DRAW 1 IN 20 SERIES

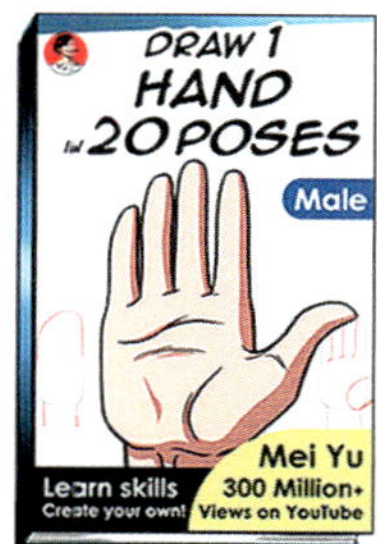

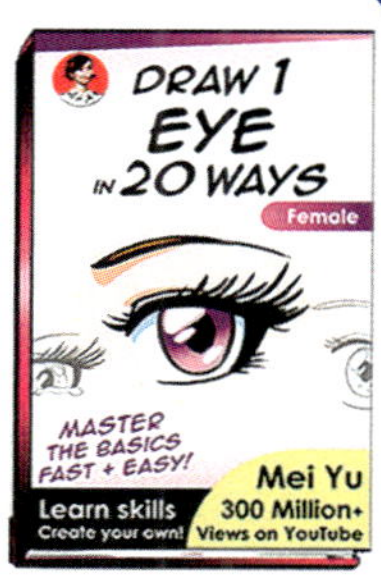
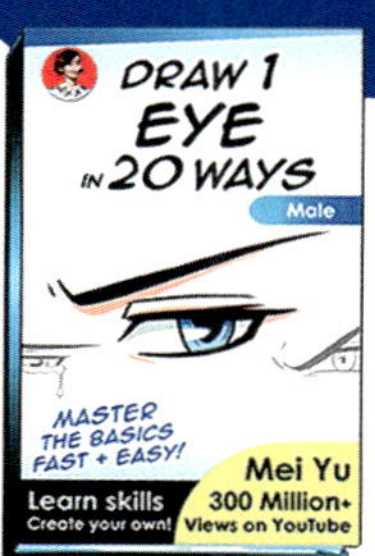

AND MORE...

★ Draw Reimagined Characters Series

AND MORE...

★ Fun2draw™ Series

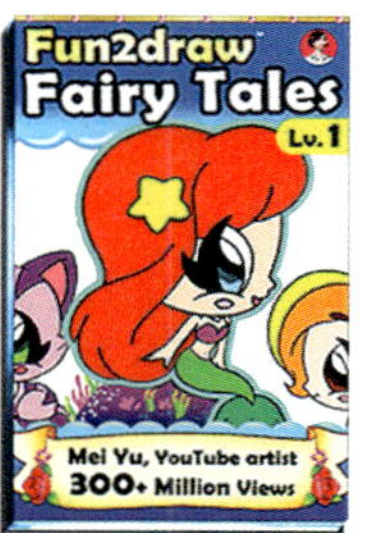
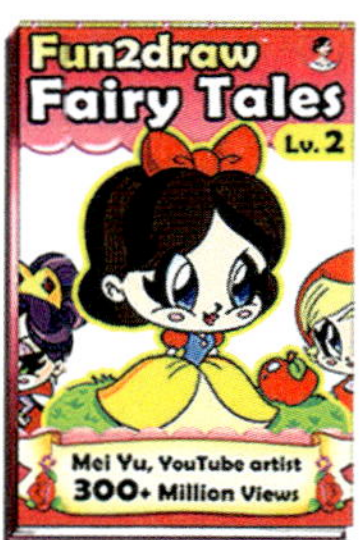

AND MORE...

Get it on iBooks

https://itunes.apple.com/us/author/mei-yu/id1055789735

available at amazon

https://www.amazon.com/shop/meiyu

Mei Yu Art

Search Amazon, Kindle, iTunes, Kobo

Android™ users: Download the Kindle App to get my eBooks

Kobo users: Search "Mei Yu Art" in the Kobo app or Kobo website

About Mei Yu

Mei Yu started drawing on walls at age 2. She is a diverse artist and designer from Canada. Mei also has a popular YouTube art channel **www.youtube.com/MeiYu** with over 1.5 million subscribers, 800 videos, and 300 million views.

Mei is happy to know that many fans are inspired by her art and books, and that they are encouraged to pursue art.

Manufactured by Amazon.ca
Bolton, ON